HIGH PROTEIN – HIGH FIBER
MEAL PREP GUIDE

100 Recipes that can create over 500 Meals

KRUPA AND KRISH

Disclaimer:

The nutritional information provided in this cookbook is intended as a general guideline only. The information is based on the ingredients and quantities used in the recipes, and it does not take into account any variations or substitutions that may be made.

Please note that the nutritional content of a dish can vary depending on the quality and brand of the ingredients used. Therefore, the values provided may not be accurate for your specific situation. We recommend that you consult a qualified nutritionist or dietitian to obtain personalized advice on your dietary needs.

While every effort has been made to ensure the accuracy of the nutritional information in this cookbook, we cannot guarantee that the values are completely error-free. The authors and publishers of this cookbook disclaim any liability or responsibility for any loss or damage that may be incurred as a result of reliance on this information.

Please use your own discretion and judgment when making any changes to your diet or nutritional intake based on the information provided in this cookbook.

We hope that you enjoy the recipes and find them to be a helpful resource for your cooking needs.

INTRODUCTION

Welcome to the High Protein-High Fiber Meal Prep Guide, a comprehensive collection of recipes designed to help you incorporate more fiber-rich foods into your daily meals. With this book, you'll discover a wide range of delicious and nutritious recipes that will not only satisfy your taste buds but also support your overall health and well-being.

In today's fast-paced world, finding time to prepare healthy meals can be a challenge. That's where meal prepping comes in. By dedicating some time to plan and prepare your meals in advance, you can save valuable time throughout the week and ensure that you have nutritious options readily available.

This book is packed with 100 diverse and flavorful recipes that will make your meal prepping journey enjoyable and convenient. From hearty breakfasts to satisfying lunches and dinners, as well as snacks and desserts, you'll find a variety of options to suit your tastes and dietary preferences.

One of the unique features of this meal prep guide is the Meal Prep Combos. We understand the importance of balancing both protein and fiber in your diet, which is why we have created combinations of recipes to help you achieve just that. Each combo starts with a high-protein recipe, followed by three high-fiber recipes that complement it perfectly. This not only ensures you're getting the necessary protein intake but also provides the essential fiber your body needs for optimal digestion and overall wellness.

By following the meal prep combos provided in this book, you can create over 500 balanced meals that are rich in both protein and fiber. Whether you're looking to maintain a healthy weight, support your digestive health, or simply make better food choices, this guide will be your go-to resource for nutritious and delicious meal prep ideas.

So, get ready to embark on a journey of flavorful and fiber-rich meals that will nourish your body and delight your taste buds. With the High Protein-High Fiber Meal Prep Guide as your companion, you'll discover how easy it can be to create wholesome, satisfying meals that support your health and well-being.

Let's dive in and begin your high-fiber meal prep adventure!

Contents

High Protein High Fiber Meals

GRILLED CHICKEN BREAST

Prep Time
10 mins

Cook Time
4 mins

Total Time
15 mins

Serving
4

Nutrition

Calories: 418 kcal, Protein: 44g,
Carbohydrate: 2g, Fat: 26g, Fiber: 0g

INGREDENTS

- 4 chicken breasts (about 200g each)
- 2 tbsp olive oil
- 2 cloves garlic, minced
- Salt and pepper to taste
- Juice of 1 lemon
- Fresh herbs (e.g., rosemary, thyme, or parsley), optional

INSTRUCTIONS

1. Preheat the grill to medium-high heat.
2. Rub the meat breasts with olive oil, then powder both sides with salt, pepper, and minced garlic. Squeeze fresh lemon juice over the meat, and sprinkle with fresh herbs if used.
3. Place the chicken on the grill and cook for 6-7 minutes on each side until the internal temperature reaches 165°F (74°C).
4. Let the chicken rest for three minutes before serving.

BLACK BEAN AND VEGETABLE CHILI

Prep Time
15 mins

Cook Time
60 mins

Total Time
1 hrs 15 minst

Serving
4

Nutrition

Calories: 450 kcal, Protein: 20g,
Carbohydrate: 70g, Fat: 10g, Fiber: 17g

INGREDENTS

- 2 cups black beans, soaked and cooked
- 2 large bell peppers, chopped
- 1 large onion, chopped
- 2 cloves of garlic, minced
- 2 tablespoons chili powder
- 1 teaspoon cumin
- Salt and pepper to taste
- 1 28 oz can crushed tomatoes
- 1 tablespoon olive oil

INSTRUCTIONS

1. In a stockpot, heat one tbsp of oil over medium heat. Add onion, chopped bell peppers, and garlic, and cook until softened.
2. Stir in chili powder, cumin, salt, and pepper.
3. Add black beans and crushed tomatoes and stir to combine. Bring to a boil.
4. Decrease the stove heat to low, cover, and simmer for one hour, stirring occasionally. Serve hot.

BEEF STIR FRY WITH RICE

Prep Time
20 mins

Cook Time
20 mins

Total Time
40 mins

Serving
4

Nutrition

Calories: 450 kcal, Protein: 45g,
Carbohydrate: 45g, Fat: 13g, Fiber: 4g

INGREDENTS

- 500g lean beef strips
- 2 tbsp olive oil
- 2 cloves garlic, minced
- 1 onion, thinly sliced
- 1 bell pepper, sliced
- 1 cup broccoli florets
- 1/4 cup soy sauce
- 1 tbsp cornstarch
- Salt and pepper to taste
- 2 cups cooked brown rice

INSTRUCTIONS

1. Heat one tbsp oil in a non-stick pan over medium-high heat. Add the beef strips, season with salt and pepper, and cook until browned. Remove from the pan and set aside.
2. Add leftover oil, garlic, onion, bell pepper, and broccoli. Stir fry until the vegetables are tender.
3. Mix the soy sauce with cornstarch in a small bowl to make a slurry. Add this to the pan with the vegetables, then return the beef to the pan. Stir well to combine, cooking for a few more minutes until everything is well coated, and the sauce has thickened.
4. Serve the beef stir fry over cooked brown rice.

LENTIL AND VEGETABLE CURRY

 Prep Time
15 mins

 Cook Time
45 mins

 Total Time
1 hour

 Serving
4

Nutrition

Calories: 460 kcal, Protein: 25g,
Carbohydrate: 75g, Fat: 8g, Fiber: 18g

INGREDENTS

- 2 cups lentils, soaked and cooked
- 1 large onion, chopped
- 2 cloves of garlic, minced
- 2 tablespoons curry powder
- Salt and pepper to taste
- 2 large carrots, diced
- 2 cups chopped broccoli
- 1 tablespoon olive oil

INSTRUCTIONS

1. Heat one tbsp oil in a non-stick frypan over medium heat. Add diced onion with minced garlic and cook until softened.
2. Add curry powder, salt, and crushed pepper.
3. Add the lentils, carrots, and broccoli, and stir to combine.
4. Cover and simmer for thirty minutes, until the vegetables are tender. Serve hot.

CHICKEN AND SHRIMP PAELLA

Prep Time
20 mins

Cook Time
40 mins

Total Time
60 mins

Serving
4

Nutrition

Calories: 400 kcal, Protein: 41g,
Carbohydrate: 38g, Fat: 7g, Fiber: 2g

INGREDENTS

- 200g chicken breast, diced
- 200g shrimp, peeled and deveined
- 1 tbsp olive oil
- 1 onion, finely chopped
- 2 cloves garlic, minced
- 1 red bell pepper, sliced
- 1 cup Arborio rice
- 1/4 tsp saffron threads
- 2 cups low-sodium chicken broth
- Salt and pepper to taste
- Fresh parsley for garnish
- Lemon wedges for serving

INSTRUCTIONS

1. Heat one tbsp oil in a non-stick skillet over medium-high heat. Add the chicken and cook until browned. Remove and set aside.
2. In the same pan, cook the shrimp until pink, then remove and set aside with the chicken.
3. Add the onion, garlic, bell pepper to the pan and sauté until softened.
4. Add the rice and saffron to the pan, stirring well.
5. Add broth and bring the mixture to a simmer. Reduce the heat to low, cover, and let the rice cook for about 20 minutes.
6. Stir in the cooked chicken and shrimp, then cover and let everything cook for another 10 minutes.
7. Powder with salt and crushed pepper, then garnish with fresh parsley. Serve with lemon wedges on the side.

QUINOA AND AVOCADO SALAD

Prep Time
15 mins

Cook Time
20 mins

Total Time
35 mins

Serving
4

Nutrition

Calories: 450 kcal, Protein: 10g,
Carbohydrate: 45g, Fat: 25g, Fiber: 15g

INGREDENTS

- 1 cup quinoa, cooked
- 2 large avocados, diced
- 1 large tomato, diced
- 1 cucumber, diced
- Juice of 1 lemon
- 2 tablespoons avocado oil
- Salt and pepper to taste

INSTRUCTIONS

1. Combine the quinoa, avocados, tomato, and cucumber in a large bowl.
2. Whisk together the lemon juice with avocado oil, salt, and pepper in a small bowl.
3. Pour the avocado-lemon dressing over the salad and toss to combine. Serve chilled.

LEAN BEEF BURGERS

Prep Time
15 mins

Cook Time
15 mins

Total Time
30 mins

Serving
4

Nutrition

Calories: 444 kcal, Protein: 40g,
Carbohydrate: 26g, Fat: 20g, Fiber: 4g

INGREDENTS

- 500g lean ground beef
- Salt and pepper to taste
- 4 whole wheat hamburger buns
- Lettuce, tomato, onion, pickles, and condiments as desired

INSTRUCTIONS

1. Preheat the grill to medium-high heat.
2. Powder the ground beef with salt and crushed pepper, then shape it into four patties.
3. Grill the patties for about 5-7 minutes on each side or until they reach your desired level of doneness.
4. Serve the burgers with whole wheat buns with your choice of toppings.

CHICKPEA AND SPINACH STEW

Prep Time
15 mins

Cook Time
45 mins

Total Time
1 hour

Serving
4

Nutrition

Calories: 380 kcal, Protein: 20g,
Carbohydrate: 60g, Fat: 8g, Fiber: 17g

INGREDENTS

- 2 cups chickpeas, soaked and cooked
- 1 large onion, chopped
- 2 cloves of garlic, minced
- 1 teaspoon cumin
- Salt and pepper to taste
- 4 cups spinach, washed
- 1 tablespoon olive oil

INSTRUCTIONS

1. In a non-stick pot, heat olive oil over medium heat. Add diced onion with garlic and cook until softened.
2. Stir in cumin, salt, and pepper.
3. Add chickpeas and spinach and stir to combine.
4. Cover and simmer for about 30 minutes, until the spinach is wilted. Serve hot.

GRILLED CHICKEN SKEWERS

Prep Time
15 mins

Cook Time
15 mins

Total Time
30 mins

Serving
4

Nutrition

Calories: 408 kcal, Protein: 46g,
Carbohydrate: 2g, Fat: 24g, Fiber: 0g

INGREDENTS

- 4 chicken breasts (about 200g each)
- Juice of 1 lemon
- 2 tbsp olive oil
- 2 cloves garlic, minced
- Salt and pepper to taste
- 1 tbsp fresh herbs (e.g., rosemary, thyme, or parsley)

INSTRUCTIONS

1. Cut the chicken into chunks, then place in a large bowl.
2. Whisk the lemon juice with olive oil, garlic, salt, pepper, and herbs in a separate bowl. Pour this marinade over the chicken and toss to coat. Cover and refrigerate for one hour.
3. Preheat the grill to medium-high heat.
4. Thread the chicken chunks onto skewers, then grill for 6-7 minutes on each side or until the chicken is cooked.
5. Serve the chicken skewers with a side of your choice.

BAKED PEARLED BARLEY AND MUSHROOM RISOTTO

Prep Time
15 mins

Cook Time
60 mins

Total Time
1 hrs 15 mins

Serving
4

Nutrition

Calories: 460 kcal, Protein: 10g,
Carbohydrate: 95g, Fat: 7g, Fiber: 16g

INGREDIENTS

- 1 cup pearled barley
- 2 cups sliced mushrooms
- 1 large onion, chopped
- 2 cloves of garlic, minced
- 4 cups vegetable broth
- 1 tablespoon olive oil
- Salt and pepper to taste

INSTRUCTIONS

1. Turn your oven heat range to 350°F (175°C).
2. Begin by warming olive oil over medium heat in a pot safe for oven use. Proceed by incorporating the onion and garlic, sautéing until they become softened.
3. After this, amalgamate the barley and mushrooms into the mixture, introducing the vegetable broth. Escalate the heat until a boil ensues.
4. Once boiling, secure the pot with its lid and relocate it to an oven that has been appropriately preheated. Bake for about 45 minutes, until the barley is tender and most of the liquid is absorbed. Serve hot.

HIGH
FIBER
★★★

BAKED LEMON AND HERB SALMON

Prep Time
10 mins

Cook Time
20 mins

Total Time
30 mins

Serving
4

Nutrition

Calories: 425 kcal, Protein: 48g,
Carbohydrate: 2g, Fat: 25g, Fiber: 0g

INGREDENTS

- 4 salmon fillets (around 200g each)
- 4 tbsp lemon juice
- 2 cloves garlic, minced
- Fresh herbs (e.g., dill, parsley), finely chopped
- 2 tbsp olive oil
- Salt and pepper to taste
- Lemon slices, for garnish

INSTRUCTIONS

1. Turn your oven heat range to 400°F (200°C). Put the salmon fillets on the paper-arranged baking tray. Rub olive oil over the fish, then season them with salt, pepper, minced garlic, and a squeeze of lemon juice. Sprinkle the chopped herbs over the top.
2. Bake for 17-20 minutes or until the salmon is cooked. Garnish with lemon slices before serving.

BROCCOLI AND BRUSSELS SPROUTS SLAW

Prep Time
20 mins

Cook Time
00 mins

Total Time
20 mins

Serving
4

Nutrition

Calories: 180 kcal, Protein: 5g,
Carbohydrate: 18g, Fat: 12g, Fiber: 15g

INGREDIENTS	INSTRUCTIONS
• 3 cups shredded broccoli stems • 3 cups shredded Brussels sprouts • 1/4 cup olive oil • Juice of 1 lemon • Salt and pepper to taste	1. In the deep-bottom bowl, combine the shredded broccoli and Brussels sprouts. 2. Whisk the 1/4 cup oil with lemon juice, salt, and crushed pepper in a small bowl. 3. Pour the lemon oil dressing over the slaw and toss to combine. Chill before serving.

BEEF AND VEGETABLE STEW

Prep Time
20 mins

Cook Time
2 hours

Total Time
2 hrs 20 mins

Serving
4

Nutrition

Calories: 440 kcal, Protein: 47g,
Carbohydrate: 18g, Fat: 20g, Fiber: 4g

INGREDENTS

- 600g lean beef stew meat, cut into chunks
- 4 tbsp olive oil
- 1 onion, chopped
- 2 cloves garlic, minced
- 3 carrots, chopped
- 3 celery stalks, chopped
- 1 cup peas
- 4 cups of low-sodium beef broth
- Salt and pepper to taste
- Fresh parsley for garnish

INSTRUCTIONS

1. Heat 4 tbsp oil in a large stockpot over medium heat. Add beef and brown on all sides. Remove from the pot and set aside.
2. Add the onion, garlic, carrots, and celery to the same pot. Sauté until softened.
3. Return the beef to the pot, then add the beef broth. Boil this mixture, then decrease the stove heat and let it simmer, covered, for about 1.5 hours.
4. Stir in the peas and let the stew cook for another half an hour. Season with salt and pepper to taste.
5. Serve the stew garnished with fresh parsley.

KALE AND QUINOA SALAD

 Prep Time
20 mins

 Cook Time
00 mins

 Total Time
20 mins

 Serving
4

Nutrition

Calories: 330 kcal, Protein: 11g,
Carbohydrate: 45g, Fat: 18g, Fiber: 16g

INGREDENTS

- 3 cups cooked quinoa
- 6 cups chopped kale
- 1/4 cup olive oil
- Juice of 1 lemon
- Salt and pepper to taste

INSTRUCTIONS

1. In a large bowl, combine the quinoa and kale.
2. Whisk the 1/4 cup oil, lemon juice, salt, and crushed pepper in a small bowl.
3. Pour the lemon oil dressing over the salad and toss to combine. Chill before serving.

BARBECUED SHRIMP SKEWERS

Prep Time
15 mins

Cook Time
10 mins

Total Time
25 mins

Serving
4

Nutrition

Calories: 405 kcal, Protein: 50g,
Carbohydrate: 15g, Fat: 15g, Fiber: 0g

INGREDENTS

- 800g shrimp, peeled and deveined
- ½ cup barbecue sauce
- 4 tbsp olive oil
- 1 clove garlic, minced
- Juice of 1 lemon

INSTRUCTIONS

1. Combine the barbecue sauce, olive oil, minced garlic, and lemon juice in a large bowl. Add the shrimp and toss to coat. Cover and refrigerate for one hour.
2. Preheat your grill to medium-high heat.
3. Thread the shrimp onto skewers, then grill for 2-3 minutes on each side until the shrimp are pink and cooked.
4. Serve the shrimp skewers with a side of your choice.

AVOCADO AND EDAMAME SALAD

Prep Time
20 mins

Cook Time
00 mins

Total Time
20 mins

Serving
4

Nutrition

Calories: 400 kcal, Protein: 15g,
Carbohydrate: 22g, Fat: 30g, Fiber: 16g

INGREDENTS	INSTRUCTIONS
• 3 cups shelled edamame • 3 large avocados, diced • 1/4 cup olive oil • Juice of 1 lemon • Salt and pepper to taste	1. In a large bowl, combine the edamame and diced avocado. 2. Beat the 1/4 cup oil with lemon juice, salt, and crushed pepper in a small bowl. 3. Drizzle the lemon oil dressing over the salad and toss to combine. Chill before serving.

LAMB MEATBALLS CURRY

 Prep Time
30 mins

 Cook Time
30 mins

 Total Time
60 mins

 Serving
4

Nutrition

Calories: 450 kcal, Protein: 41g,
Carbohydrate: 8g, Fat: 29g, Fiber: 2g

INGREDENTS

- 500g ground lamb
- 1 onion, finely chopped
- 2 cloves garlic, minced
- 2 tbsp curry powder
- 1 can of coconut milk
- 1 tbsp olive oil
- Salt and pepper to taste

INSTRUCTIONS

1. Combine the ground lamb, half of the chopped onion, one minced garlic clove, and 1 tbsp curry powder in a large bowl. Season with salt and pepper. Roll the mixture into meatballs.
2. Heat one tbsp oil in a non-stick skillet over moderate heat. Add meatballs and cook until done on all sides. Remove and set aside.
3. In the same skillet, add the remaining onion and garlic. Sauté until softened, then stir in the remaining curry powder. Add coconut milk and boil the mixture.
4. Return the meatballs to the skillet and let them simmer in the curry sauce for about 20 minutes or until cooked.
5. Serve the lamb meatballs curry with a side of your choice.

BEET AND LENTIL SALAD

 Prep Time
20 mins

 Cook Time
00 mins

 Total Time
20 mins

 Serving
4

Nutrition

Calories: 360 kcal, Protein: 18g,
Carbohydrate: 45g, Fat: 14g, Fiber: 15g

INGREDENTS	INSTRUCTIONS
<ul><li>2 cups cooked lentils</li><li>2 large beets, roasted and diced</li><li>1/4 cup olive oil</li><li>2 tbsp apple cider vinegar</li><li>Salt and pepper to taste</li></ul>	1. In a large bowl, combine the lentils and diced beets. 2. Whisk together the olive oil with apple cider vinegar, salt, and crushed pepper in a small bowl. 3. Pour the vinegar oil dressing over the salad and toss to combine. Chill before serving.

HIGH
FIBER
★★★

HONEY MUSTARD GLAZED GRILLED CHICKEN THIGHS

Prep Time
10 mins

Cook Time
15 mins

Total Time
25 mins

Serving
4

Nutrition

Calories: 422 kcal, Protein: 42g,
Carbohydrate: 18g, Fat: 20g, Fiber: 1g

INGREDENTS

- 8 boneless, skinless chicken thighs (around 500g total)
- 1/4 cup honey
- 1/4 cup Dijon mustard
- 2 tbsp olive oil
- Salt and pepper to taste

INSTRUCTIONS

1. Combine the honey, Dijon mustard, olive oil, salt, and pepper in a large bowl. Add meat thighs and toss to coat. Cover and refrigerate for one hour.
2. Preheat your grill to medium-high heat.
3. Grill the chicken thighs on each side for 6-7 minutes until thoroughly cooked.
4. Serve the chicken thighs with a side of your choice.

CHIA SEED PUDDING WITH BERRIES

Prep Time
10 mins

Cook Time
00 mins

Total Time
10 mins

Serving
4

Nutrition

Calories: 210 kcal, Protein: 5g,
Carbohydrate: 35g, Fat: 8g, Fiber: 15g

INGREDIENTS	INSTRUCTIONS
• 1/4 cup chia seeds • 1 cup almond milk • 1 tablespoon honey • 1 cup mixed berries	1. Combine the chia seeds, almond milk, and honey in a bowl. 2. Stir well and refrigerate overnight. 3. Before serving, top with mixed berries.

HIGH FIBER
★★★

SMOKED SEA BASS WITH HERBS

Prep Time
10 mins

Cook Time
25 mins

Total Time
35 mins

Serving
4

Nutrition

Calories: 436 kcal, Protein: 47g,
Carbohydrate: 8g, Fat: 24g, Fiber: 0g

INGREDENTS	INSTRUCTIONS
• 4 sea bass fillets (around 200g each) • 2 bunch fresh herbs (e.g., dill, parsley, rosemary) • 4 tbsp olive oil • Salt and pepper to taste	1. Preheat your smoke according to the manufacturer's instructions. 2. Rub the sea bass fillets with olive oil, then season with salt and pepper. Arrange the herbs over the top. 3. Smoke the sea bass for about 20-25 minutes until it flakes easily with a fork. 4. Serve the smoked sea bass with a side of your choice.

ROASTED SWEET POTATO AND QUINOA SALAD

 Prep Time
15 mins

 Cook Time
30 mins

 Total Time
45 mins

 Serving
4

Nutrition

Calories: 480 kcal, Protein: 12g,
Carbohydrate: 102g, Fat: 6g, Fiber: 16g

INGREDENTS

- 4 large, sweet potatoes, peeled and diced
- 4 cups cooked quinoa
- 2 tbsp olive oil
- Salt and pepper to taste

INSTRUCTIONS

1. Turn your oven heat range to 400°F (200°C).
2. Toss the diced sweet potatoes in olive oil, salt, and pepper.
3. Spread the dice sweet potato baking sheet and roast for thirty minutes until golden and soft.
4. Mix the cooked quinoa and roasted sweet potatoes, season as needed, and serve warm or cold.

ROASTED BEEF WITH GARLIC AND ROSEMARY

Prep Time
10 mins

Cook Time
1 hour

Total Time
1 hrs 10 mins

Serving
4

Nutrition

Calories: 407 kcal, Protein: 48g,
Carbohydrate: 1g, Fat: 22g, Fiber: 0g

INGREDENTS	INSTRUCTIONS
• 600g lean beef roast • 5 cloves garlic, minced • 2 sprigs of fresh rosemary • 3 tbsp olive oil • Salt and pepper to taste	1. Turn your oven heat to 375°F (190°C). 2. Rub the beef roast with olive oil, then season with salt, pepper, and minced garlic. Arrange the rosemary sprigs over the top. 3. Roast the beef for one hour. 4. Cool for three minutes before slicing and serving.

CHICKPEA AND TOMATO SALAD WITH LEMON DRESSING

 Prep Time
15 mins

 Cook Time
00 mins

 Total Time
15 mins

 Serving
4

Nutrition

Calories: 400 kcal, Protein: 20g,
Carbohydrate: 68g, Fat: 8g, Fiber: 20g

INGREDENTS

- 4 cups cooked chickpeas
- 2 large tomatoes, diced
- 2 tbsp lime juice
- 1 tbsp apple cider vinegar
- 2 tbsp olive oil
- Salt and pepper to taste

INSTRUCTIONS

1. In a bowl, combine the chickpeas and diced tomatoes.
2. Whisk together the lime juice with apple cider vinegar, olive oil, salt, and crushed pepper in a separate bowl.
3. Pour the lime vinegar dressing over the salad and toss to combine.
4. Chill before serving.

GARLIC BUTTER BAKED SALMON

Prep Time
10 mins

Cook Time
20 mins

Total Time
30 mins

Serving
4

Nutrition

Calories: 415 kcal, Protein: 49g,
Carbohydrate: 1g, Fat: 23g, Fiber: 0g

INGREDENTS

- 4 salmon fillets (around 200g each)
- 3 cloves garlic, minced
- 2 tbsp butter, melted
- Fresh herbs (e.g., dill, parsley) for garnish
- Salt and pepper to taste

INSTRUCTIONS

1. Turn your oven heat range to 400°F (200°C).
2. Put the salmon fillets in a baking dish. Season with salt, pepper, and minced garlic, then drizzle the melted butter over the top.
3. Bake for 17-20 minutes until it flakes easily with a fork.
4. Garnish with fresh herbs before serving.

CAULIFLOWER FRIED RICE

Prep Time
15 mins

Cook Time
15 mins

Total Time
30 mins

Serving
4

Nutrition

Calories: 210 kcal, Protein: 10g,
Carbohydrate: 40g, Fat: 5g, Fiber: 16g

INGREDENTS

- 2 large head cauliflower, riced
- 1 cup frozen peas
- 1 cup diced carrots
- 2 tbsp sesame oil
- Salt and pepper to taste

INSTRUCTIONS

1. Heat two tbsp sesame oil in a large skillet over medium heat.
2. Add the riced cauliflower, peas, and carrots.
3. Stir-fry for about 10 minutes until the vegetables are tender.
4. Season with salt and crushed pepper and serve warm.

HIGH
FIBER
★★★

BEEF RENDANG

Prep Time
20 mins

Cook Time
2 hours

Total Time
2 hrs 20 mins

Serving
4

Nutrition

Calories: 470 kcal, Protein: 42g,
Carbohydrate: 8g, Fat: 30g, Fiber: 2g

INGREDENTS

- 500g lean beef, cut into chunks
- 1 can of coconut milk
- 2 tbsp rendang curry paste
- 1 tbsp olive oil
- Salt to taste

INSTRUCTIONS

1. Heat one tbsp oil in a large stockpot over medium heat. Add curry paste and sauté until fragrant.
2. Add beef pieces and cook until brown on all sides.
3. Add coconut milk and take it to a simmer. Decrease the stove heat to low, cover, and let it simmer for about 2 hours or until the beef is tender and the sauce has thickened.
4. Season with salt to taste before serving.

MUSHROOM AND SPINACH CAULIFLOWER RISOTTO

Prep Time
15 mins

Cook Time
20 mins

Total Time
35 mins

Serving
4

Nutrition

Calories: 250 kcal, Protein: 10g,
Carbohydrate: 35g, Fat: 9g, Fiber: 15g

INGREDIENTS

- 2 large head cauliflower, riced
- 2 cups sliced mushrooms
- 4 cups spinach
- 2 tbsp olive oil
- Salt and pepper to taste

INSTRUCTIONS

1. Heat two tbsp oil in a large skillet over medium heat.
2. Add the riced cauliflower and sliced mushrooms.
3. Cook for 7-10 minutes until the mushrooms are browned and the cauliflower is tender.
4. Add spinach and cook for two minutes until wilted.
5. Powder it with salt and crushed pepper and serve warm.

SMOKY BBQ BEEF BRISKET

Prep Time
10 mins

Cook Time
4 hours

Total Time
4 hrs 10 mins

Serving
4

Nutrition

Calories: 427 kcal, Protein: 44g,
Carbohydrate: 18g, Fat: 20g, Fiber: 1g

INGREDENTS	INSTRUCTIONS
• 500g beef brisket • ¼ cup BBQ rub • 1 cup low-sodium beef broth • ¼ cup BBQ sauce • 2 tbsp honey (optional)	1. Preheat your smoke according to the manufacturer's instructions. Rub the beef brisket all over with the BBQ rub. Smoke the brisket for about 3 hours. 2. Transfer the brisket to a baking dish. Add beef broth into the bottom of the dish with tbsp honey, then cover with foil. 3. Smoke the brisket for another hour or until the meat is tender. 4. Rest the brisket rest for a few minutes before slicing. Drizzle with BBQ sauce before serving.

BROWN RICE AND VEGETABLE STIR-FRY

Prep Time
15 mins

Cook Time
30 mins

Total Time
45 mins

Serving
4

Nutrition

Calories: 345 kcal, Protein: 8g,
Carbohydrate: 65g, Fat: 7g, Fiber: 15g

INGREDENTS

- 2 cups brown rice, cooked
- 1 cup mixed vegetables (carrots, bell peppers, peas)
- 2 tbsp sesame oil
- Salt and crushed pepper to taste

INSTRUCTIONS

1. Prepare the brown rice as directed by package instructions and set aside.
2. Heat two tbsp sesame oil in a large non-stick skillet over medium heat.
3. Add the cooked brown rice and mixed vegetables.
4. Stir-fry for about 10 minutes until the vegetables are tender.
5. Powder it with salt and crushed pepper and serve warm.

GRILLED SEA BASS WITH LEMON AND DILL

Prep Time
10 mins

Cook Time
15 mins

Total Time
25 mins

Serving
4

Nutrition

Calories: 407 kcal, Protein: 48g,
Carbohydrate: 5g, Fat: 23g, Fiber: 2g

INGREDENTS	INSTRUCTIONS
• 4 sea bass fillets (around 200g each) • 2 lemons, sliced • 1 bunch of fresh dill • 4 tbsp olive oil • Salt and pepper to taste	1. Preheat your grill to medium-high heat. 2. Rub the sea bass fillets with olive oil, then season with salt and pepper. Arrange the lemon slices and dill over the top. 3. Grill the sea bass on each side for 7-8 minutes until it flakes easily with a fork. 4. Serve the grilled sea bass with a side of your choice.

BLACK BEAN AND CORN SALAD

Prep Time
15 mins

Cook Time
00 mins

Total Time
15 mins

Serving
4

Nutrition

Calories: 350 kcal, Protein: 20g,
Carbohydrate: 65g, Fat: 2g, Fiber: 20g

INGREDENTS

- 2 cans (15 oz weight) of black beans, rinsed and drained
- 1 can (15 oz) corn, drained
- 1 large red bell pepper, diced
- 1 large green bell pepper, diced
- Juice of 2 limes
- Salt and pepper to taste

INSTRUCTIONS

1. Combine the black beans, corn, and bell peppers in a large bowl.
2. Squeeze over the lime juice, powder with salt and crushed pepper, and toss well to combine.
3. Chill for one hour (at least) before serving to allow the flavors to meld together.

SOUL FOOD JERK CHICKEN

Prep Time
15 mins

Cook Time
25 mins

Total Time
40 mins

Serving
4

Nutrition

Calories: 410 kcal, Protein: 50g,
Carbohydrate: 20g, Fat: 15g, Fiber: 1g

INGREDENTS	INSTRUCTIONS
• 4 boneless, skinless chicken breasts (around 500g total) • 1/4 cup jerk seasoning • 2 tbsp honey • 2 tbsp soy sauce • 2 tbsp olive oil	1. Combine the jerk seasoning, honey, soy sauce, and olive oil in a large bowl. Add meat breasts and toss to coat. Cover and refrigerate for one hour. 2. Preheat your grill to medium-high heat. 3. Grill the chicken breasts for 10-12 minutes for each side. 4. Serve the jerk chicken with a side of your choice.

HIGH
PROTEIN

CAULIFLOWER RICE AND BLACK BEAN BURRITO BOWL

Prep Time
15 mins

Total Time
30 mins

Serving
4

Cook Time
15 mins

Nutrition

Calories: 425 kcal, Protein: 20g,
Carbohydrate: 75g, Fat: 9g, Fiber: 35g

INGREDIENTS	INSTRUCTIONS
• 1 large head cauliflower, riced • 2 cans (15 oz weight) of black beans, rinsed and drained • 1 cup corn • 1 large avocado, sliced • Salt and pepper to taste	1. Prepare the cauliflower rice in a non-stick skillet with some oil until tender. 2. Divide the cooked cauliflower rice between 4 bowls. 3. Top each bowl with equal black beans, corn, and avocado slices. 4. Powder with salt and crushed pepper to taste and serve.

BAKED COD WITH OLIVE TAPENADE

 Prep Time
10 mins

 Cook Time
15 mins

 Total Time
25 mins

 Serving
4

Nutrition

Calories: 412 kcal, Protein: 44g,
Carbohydrate: 5g, Fat: 24g, Fiber: 3g

INGREDENTS

- 4 cod fillets (around 231g each)
- 1/4 cup olive tapenade
- 4 tbsp olive oil
- 1/4 cup almond slivers
- Salt and pepper to taste

INSTRUCTIONS

1. Turn your oven heat range to 400°F (200°C).
2. Put the cod fillets in a baking dish. Powder with salt and pepper, then spread the olive tapenade and almond slivers over the top.
3. Drizzle the fillets with olive oil and bake for 13-15 minutes until the fish flakes easily with a fork.
4. Serve the baked cod with a side of your choice.

KONJAC RICE WITH LENTILS AND VEGETABLES

Prep Time
15 mins

Cook Time
20 mins

Total Time
35 mins

Serving
4

Nutrition

Calories: 300 kcal, Protein: 20g,
Carbohydrate: 50g, Fat: 5g, Fiber: 15g

INGREDENTS	INSTRUCTIONS
• 2 packages (7oz each) of Konjac rice • 2 cups cooked lentils • 1 cup mixed vegetables (carrots, bell peppers, peas) • 2 tbsp olive oil • Salt and pepper to taste	1. Rinse the Konjac rice under warm water for a few minutes to remove the natural aroma. 2. Heat two tbsp oil in a large skillet over medium heat. 3. Add the Konjac rice, cooked lentils, and mixed vegetables. 4. Stir-fry for about 10 minutes until the vegetables are tender. 5. Season with salt and crushed pepper and serve warm.

LAMB ROGAN JOSH

 Prep Time
20 mins

 Cook Time
1 hour

 Total Time
1 hrs 20 mins

 Serving
4

Nutrition

Calories: 500 kcal, Protein: 42g,
Carbohydrate: 13g, Fat: 32g, Fiber: 3g

INGREDENTS	INSTRUCTIONS
<ul><li>500g lean lamb, cut into chunks</li><li>2 tbsp rogan josh curry paste</li><li>1 can diced tomatoes</li><li>1 cup full-fat Greek yogurt</li><li>3 tsp olive oil</li><li>Salt to taste</li></ul>	1. Heat 3 tsp oil in a non-stick pan over medium heat. Add lamb and brown on all sides. 2. Add curry paste and cook for another three minutes. 3. Add canned diced tomatoes and bring the mixture to a simmer. Decrease the stove heat to low, keep covered, and simmer for about one hour until the lamb is tender. 4. Add Greek yogurt and season with salt to taste before serving.

MUSHROOM AND BROWN RICE RISOTTO

 Prep Time
15 mins

 Cook Time
45 mins

 Total Time
60 mins

 Serving
4

Nutrition

Calories: 365 kcal, Protein: 10g,
Carbohydrate: 65g, Fat: 9g, Fiber: 15g

INGREDENTS

- 1 cup brown rice
- 2 cups sliced mushrooms
- 1 onion, diced
- 2 cloves garlic, minced
- 4 cups vegetable broth
- 2 tbsp olive oil
- Salt and pepper to taste

INSTRUCTIONS

1. Warm the olive oil in a sizeable pot, maintaining medium heat.
2. Then, integrate the onion and garlic, allowing them to cook until ttheir aroma is perceptible. Subsequently, incorporate the mushrooms into the pot, ensuring they're cooked until brown.
3. Add the rice and cook for a few more minutes.
4. Gradually add the vegetable broth, stirring continuously, until the rice is tender and creamy.
5. Powder with salt and crushed pepper and serve warm.

HIGH FIBER
★★★

BAKED CHICKEN WITH SUN-DRIED TOMATO CREAM SAUCE

Prep Time
15 mins

Cook Time
30 mins

Total Time
45 mins

Serving
4

Nutrition

Calories: 480 kcal, Protein: 50g,
Carbohydrate: 8g, Fat: 28g, Fiber: 1g

INGREDENTS

- 4 boneless, skinless chicken breasts (around 500g total)
- ¼ cup sun-dried tomatoes, chopped
- 1 cup full-fat cream
- 1 tbsp olive oil
- Salt and pepper to taste

INSTRUCTIONS

1. Turn your oven heat range to 375°F (190°C).
2. In an oven-safe pan, heat one tbsp of oil over medium heat. Powder it with salt and pepper, then add to the pan. Cook until both sides are brown, then remove from the pan.
3. In the same pan, add the sun-dried tomatoes and cream. Bring to a simmer.
4. Return the chicken breasts to the pan. Bake for 23-25 minutes until the chicken and the sauce are bubbly.
5. Serve the chicken with the sun-dried tomato cream sauce.

THREE BEAN SALAD

Prep Time
15 mins

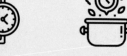

Cook Time
20 mins

Total Time
35 mins

Serving
4

Nutrition

Calories: 365 kcal, Protein: 20g,
Carbohydrate: 65g, Fat: 3g, Fiber: 20g

INGREDENTS

- 1 can (15 oz) kidney beans, rinsed and drained
- 1 can (15 oz) garbanzo beans, rinsed and drained
- 1 can (15 oz) green beans, drained
- 1 large red onion, diced
- Juice of 1 lemon
- Salt and pepper to taste

INSTRUCTIONS

1. Combine the kidney beans, garbanzo beans, green beans, and red onion in a large bowl.
2. Squeeze the fresh lemon juice, then season with salt and crushed pepper, and toss well to combine.
3. Chill in the fridge for one hour (at least) before serving.

BEEF BOURGUIGNON

Prep Time
30 mins

Cook Time
2 hours

Total Time
2 hrs 30 mins

Serving
4

Nutrition

Calories: 480 kcal, Protein: 45g,
Carbohydrate: 8g, Fat: 30g, Fiber: 2g

INGREDENTS	INSTRUCTIONS
<ul><li>700g lean beef, cut into chunks</li><li>1 cup red wine</li><li>2 carrots, sliced</li><li>2 onions, chopped</li><li>2 cloves garlic, minced</li><li>2 tbsp olive oil</li><li>Salt and pepper to taste</li></ul>	1. In a non-stick stockpot, heat two tbsp oil over medium heat. Add beef and brown on all sides. 2. Add onions, sliced carrots, and garlic to the pot. Cook for 2-3 minutes. 3. Pour in the red wine, then season with salt and pepper. Cover and simmer for two hours (at least) until the beef is tender. 4. Serve the Beef Bourguignon with a side of your choice.

KIDNEY BEAN AND CABBAGE SLAW

Prep Time
15 mins

Cook Time
00 mins

Total Time
15 mins

Serving
4

Nutrition

Calories: 350 kcal, Protein: 20g,
Carbohydrate: 55g, Fat: 8g, Fiber: 18g

INGREDENTS

- 4 cups shredded cabbage
- 2 cans (15 oz each) of kidney beans, rinsed and drained
- 2 tbsp olive oil
- 1 tbsp apple cider vinegar
- Salt and pepper to taste

INSTRUCTIONS

1. In the deep-bottom bowl, combine the shredded cabbage and kidney beans.
2. Drizzle over the two tbsp olive oil and apple cider vinegar.
3. Season with salt and crushed pepper and toss well to combine.
4. Chill for one hour (at least) before serving.

CHICKEN MARSALA

Prep Time
10 mins

Cook Time
25 mins

Total Time
35 mins

Serving
4

Nutrition

Calories: 410 kcal, Protein: 50g,
Carbohydrate: 10g, Fat: 15g, Fiber: 1g

INGREDENTS

- 4 chicken breasts (without skin & bone) (around 500g total)
- 1 cup Marsala wine
- 1 cup sliced mushrooms
- 2 tbsp olive oil
- Salt and pepper to taste

INSTRUCTIONS

1. Heat two tbsp oil in a frypan over medium heat. Rub the meat breasts with salt and pepper, then add to the pan. Cook until both sides are browned, then remove from the pan.
2. In the frypan, add mushrooms and cook for 2-3 minutes.
3. Add Marsala wine and put it to a simmer. Return the chicken to the pan and simmer for about 10-15 minutes until the chicken is cooked through.
4. Serve the Chicken Marsala with a side of your choice.

BUTTERNUT SQUASH AND BLACK BEAN STEW

Prep Time
15 mins

Cook Time
30 mins

Total Time
45 mins

Serving
4

Nutrition

Calories: 425 kcal, Protein: 20g,
Carbohydrate: 70g, Fat: 8g, Fiber: 20g

INGREDENTS

- 2 cups cubed butternut squash
- 2 cans (15 oz weight) of black beans, rinsed and drained
- 1 large onion, diced
- 2 cloves garlic, minced
- 4 cups vegetable broth
- 2 tbsp olive oil
- Salt and crushed pepper to taste

INSTRUCTIONS

1. Start by warming olive oil in a big pot set at medium heat.
2. Then, introduce onion and garlic to the pot, cooking them until their aroma becomes noticeable.
3. Proceed by mixing in butternut squash and black beans in the pot. Once mixed, cover the ingredients with vegetable broth, boil this mixture, and lower the heat, allowing it to simmer until the butternut squash softens.
4. Conclude by seasoning the dish with salt and pepper, and serve it while still warm.

GRILLED LAMB CHOPS WITH MINT SAUCE

 Prep Time 15 mins

 Cook Time 15 mins

 Total Time 30 mins

 Serving 4

Nutrition

Calories: 500 kcal, Protein: 48g,
Carbohydrate: 8g, Fat: 32g, Fiber: 1g

INGREDENTS

- 8 lamb chops (around 900g total)
- 2 tbsp olive oil
- Salt and pepper to taste
- For the Mint Sauce:
- 1 cup fresh mint leaves
- ½ cup white wine vinegar
- 2 tbsp sugar

INSTRUCTIONS

1. Rub the lamb chops with olive oil, then season with salt and pepper. Let them marinate for at least 1 hour.
2. For the Mint Sauce, blend the mint leaves, white wine vinegar, and sugar in a food processor until smooth.
3. Preheat your grill to medium-high heat. Grill the lamb chops for 5-7 minutes on each side or until they reach your desired level of doneness.
4. Serve the Grilled Lamb Chops with the Mint Sauce on the side.

CHICKPEA AND BROCCOLI STIR-FRY

Prep Time
15 mins

Cook Time
15 mins

Total Time
30 mins

Serving
4

Nutrition

Calories: 425 kcal, Protein: 20g,
Carbohydrate: 65g, Fat: 12g, Fiber: 17g

INGREDIENTS

- 2 cans (15 oz each) of chickpeas, rinsed and drained
- 4 cups chopped broccoli
- 1 large onion, diced
- 2 cloves garlic, minced
- 2 tbsp olive oil
- Salt and pepper to taste

INSTRUCTIONS

1. Heat two tbsp oil in the non-stick frypan over moderate heat. Add diced onion with minced garlic and cook until fragrant.
2. Stir in the chickpeas and broccoli.
3. Cook, stirring frequently, until the broccoli is tenderer.
4. Season with crushed salt and pepper and serve warm.

SMOKED SALMON WITH DILL SAUCE

Prep Time
2 hours

Cook Time
4 hours

Total Time
6 hours

Serving
4

Nutrition

Calories: 400 kcal, Protein: 42g,
Carbohydrate: 6g, Fat: 25g, Fiber: 0g

INGREDENTS

- 400g salmon fillet, skin on
- 1/4 cup salt (for the brine)
- 1/4 cup brown sugar (for the brine)
- For the Dill Sauce:
- 1 cup Greek yogurt
- 1 tbsp fresh dill
- 1 tbsp lemon juice
- Salt and pepper to taste

INSTRUCTIONS

1. Mix salt and brown sugar in a shallow dish, then add the salmon fillet, ensuring the brine mixture covers it fully. Let it rest in the refrigerator for at least 2 hours or overnight for a stronger flavor.
2. Preheat your smoker to about 150°F (65°C).
3. Rinse the brine off the salmon under room temperature water and pat dry with a paper towel. Let it rest at room temperature for an hour to form a pellicle (a thin skin that helps the smoke adhere to the fish).
4. Smoke the salmon on the preheated smoker for approximately 3 to 4 hours until its internal temperature almost touches the 145°F (63°C).
5. While the salmon is smoking, prepare the dill sauce by mixing the Greek yogurt, fresh dill, lemon juice, salt, and crushed pepper in a bowl. Adjust the seasonings to taste.
6. Serve the smoked salmon with the dill sauce on the side.

APPLE, WALNUT AND MIXED GREENS SALAD

Prep Time
15 mins

Cook Time
00 mins

Total Time
15 mins

Serving
4

Nutrition

Calories: 480 kcal, Protein: 10g,
Carbohydrate: 40g, Fat: 32g, Fiber: 15g

INGREDIENTS

- 8 cups mixed greens
- 3 large apples, cored and chopped
- 1.5 cups walnuts, chopped
- 2 tbsp olive oil
- 1 tbsp apple cider vinegar
- Salt and pepper to taste

INSTRUCTIONS

1. Combine the mixed greens, apples, and walnuts in a large bowl.
2. Drizzle over the two tbsp olive oil and apple cider vinegar.
3. Season with salt and crushed pepper and toss well to combine.
4. Serve immediately.

HIGH
FIBER
★★★

CHICKEN SOUVLAKI WITH TZATZIKI SAUCE

Prep Time
20 mins

Cook Time
10 mins

Total Time
30 mins

Serving
4

Nutrition

Calories: 450 kcal, Protein: 50g,
Carbohydrate: 10g, Fat: 23g, Fiber: 1g

INGREDENTS

- 4 boneless, skinless chicken breasts (around 500g total)
- 2 tbsp olive oil
- 1 tbsp lemon juice
- 1 tbsp dried oregano
- Salt and pepper to taste
- For the Tzatziki Sauce:
- 1 cup Greek yogurt
- ½ cucumber (grated and drained)
- 2 cloves garlic (minced)
- 1 tbsp fresh dill
- 1 tbsp lemon juice
- Salt and pepper to taste

INSTRUCTIONS

1. Rub the chicken breasts with olive oil, lemon juice, dried oregano, salt, and pepper. Let them marinate for at least 1 hour.
2. For the Tzatziki Sauce, whisk all the ingredients in a bowl.
3. Preheat your grill to medium-high heat. Grill the meat breasts for about 5 minutes on each side or until cooked through.
4. Serve the Chicken Souvlaki with the Tzatziki Sauce on the side.

BROCCOLI AND ALMOND SLAW

Prep Time
15 mins

Cook Time
00 mins

Total Time
15 mins

Serving
4

Nutrition

Calories: 480 kcal, Protein: 18g,
Carbohydrate: 20g, Fat: 40g, Fiber: 17g

INGREDENTS	INSTRUCTIONS
• 6 cups shredded broccoli • 2 cups sliced almonds • 2 tbsp olive oil • 1 tbsp apple cider vinegar • Salt and pepper to taste	1. In the deep-bottom bowl, combine the shredded broccoli and sliced almonds. 2. Drizzle over the 2 tbsp olive oil and apple cider vinegar. 3. Powder with salt and crushed pepper and toss well to combine. 4. Chill for 1 hour (at least) before serving to allow the flavors to meld together.

BARBECUED OYSTERS

Prep Time
10 mins

Cook Time
10 mins

Total Time
20 mins

Serving
4

Nutrition

Calories: 410 kcal, Protein: 42g,
Carbohydrate: 8g, Fat: 24g, Fiber: 0g

INGREDENTS

- 24 oysters
- 1/4 cup butter, melted
- 1 tbsp lemon juice
- 1 tbsp chopped fresh parsley
- Salt and pepper to taste

INSTRUCTIONS

1. Preheat your grill to high heat.
2. Shuck the oysters and leave them on the half-shell. Place them on the grill.
3. Mix the melted butter, lemon juice, parsley, salt, and pepper in a bowl. Drizzle this mixture over the oysters.
4. Grill the oysters for about 5-10 minutes or until they are cooked.
5. Serve the Barbecued Oysters with additional lemon wedges, if desired.

ROASTED BRUSSELS SPROUTS AND CHICKPEA SALAD

Prep Time
10 mins

Cook Time
20 mins

Total Time
30 mins

Serving
4

Nutrition

Calories: 440 kcal, Protein: 17g,
Carbohydrate: 56g, Fat: 16g, Fiber: 15g

INGREDIENTS

- 4 cups Brussels sprouts, halved
- 1 can (15 oz weight) chickpeas, drained and rinsed
- 2 tablespoons olive oil
- Salt and pepper to taste
- 2 tablespoons balsamic vinegar
- 2 tablespoons Dijon mustard

INSTRUCTIONS

1. Turn your oven heat range to 400°F (200°C).
2. Toss the Brussels sprouts and chickpeas with the olive oil, salt, and pepper.
3. Spread the Brussels sprouts and chickpeas on the baking sheet and roast for 19-20 minutes.
4. Whisk the balsamic vinegar with Dijon mustard to make a dressing.
5. Toss the roasted vegetables with the dressing and serve.

HIGH
FIBER
★★★

BAKED BEEF MEATBALLS IN TOMATO SAUCE

Prep Time
20 mins

Cook Time
40 mins

Total Time
60 mins

Serving
4

Nutrition

Calories: 480 kcal, Protein: 48g,
Carbohydrate: 20g, Fat: 24g, Fiber: 4g

INGREDIENTS	INSTRUCTIONS
• 500g lean ground beef • 1 cup breadcrumbs • 1 egg • 2 cups tomato sauce • Salt and pepper to taste	1. Turn your oven heat range to 375°F (190°C). 2. Mix the ground beef, breadcrumbs, egg, salt, and pepper in a bowl. Form this mixture into meatballs and place them in a baking dish. 3. Pour the tomato sauce over the meatballs. 4. Bake for 30-40 minutes or until the meatballs are cooked. 5. Serve the Baked Beef Meatballs in Tomato Sauce with a side of your choice.

VEGETABLE AND BLACK BEAN ENCHILADAS

Prep Time
20 mins

Cook Time
25 mins

Total Time
45 mins

Serving
4

Nutrition

Calories: 500 kcal, Protein: 21g,
Carbohydrate: 80g, Fat: 12g, Fiber: 19g

INGREDENTS

- 8 whole grain tortillas
- 2 cans (15 oz weight) of black beans, drained and rinsed
- 2 cups chopped bell peppers
- 2 cups frozen corn
- 1 jar (16 oz) enchilada sauce
- 1 cup shredded cheese
- 1 cup diced tomatoes
- ½ cup chopped cilantro

INSTRUCTIONS

1. Turn your oven heat range to 375°F (190°C). Mix the black beans, bell peppers, corn, tomatoes, and half of the enchilada sauce in a bowl.
2. Spread a layer (a thin layer) of enchilada sauce. Fill each tortilla with the vegetable and bean mixture, roll it up, and place seam-side down in the baking dish.
3. Top with leftover enchilada sauce and sprinkle with cheese. Bake for 23-25 minutes until the cheese melts completely. Garnish with cilantro before serving.

GRILLED LOBSTER TAILS WITH GARLIC BUTTER

Prep Time
15 mins

Cook Time
15 mins

Total Time
30 mins

Serving
4

Nutrition

Calories: 450 kcal, Protein: 40g,
Carbohydrate: 2g, Fat: 30g, Fiber: 0g

INGREDENTS

- 4 lobster tails
- 1/4 cup butter, melted
- 2 cloves garlic, minced
- Salt and pepper to taste

INSTRUCTIONS

1. Preheat your grill to medium-high heat.
2. Cut the lobster tails in half lengthwise. Mix the melted butter, garlic, salt, and pepper in a bowl.
3. Rub the lobster tails with the garlic butter, then place them on the grill, shell side down.
4. Grill for 5-7 minutes until the lobster meat is opaque and cooked.
5. Serve the Grilled Lobster Tails with additional garlic butter on the side.

BAKED SWEET POTATO AND LENTIL PATTIES

 Prep Time
10 mins

 Cook Time
20 mins

 Total Time
30 mins

 Serving
4

Nutrition

Calories: 480 kcal, Protein: 20g,
Carbohydrate: 82g, Fat: 6g, Fiber: 18g

INGREDENTS

- 2 cups cooked lentils
- 2 cups cooked and mashed sweet potato
- 1/2 cup rolled oats
- 2 cloves garlic, minced
- Salt and pepper to taste

INSTRUCTIONS

1. Turn your oven heat range to 375°F (190°C).
2. Combine the lentils, sweet potato, oats, and garlic in a large bowl. Season with salt and pepper.
3. Form into patties and place on a baking sheet.
4. Bake for 17-20 minutes until firm and golden.
5. Serve with a salad or on a whole-grain bun.

BEEF STEAK DIANE

Prep Time
10 mins

Cook Time
20 mins

Total Time
30 mins

Serving
4

Nutrition

Calories: 460 kcal, Protein: 45g,
Carbohydrate: 2g, Fat: 30g, Fiber: 0g

INGREDENTS

- 4 beef steaks (around 500g total)
- 2 tbsp butter
- 1/4 cup brandy
- 1 cup beef stock
- Salt and pepper to taste

INSTRUCTIONS

1. Heat two tbsp butter in a frypan over medium-high heat. Powder the steaks with salt and crushed pepper, then cook them in the pan for about 5 minutes on each side or until they are cooked to your liking. Remove the steaks from the pan and set them aside.
2. Drizzle the pan with the brandy, scraping the browned bits from the sides and bottom. Add the beef stock and let it simmer for about 10 minutes, or until the sauce has reduced by half.
3. Return the steaks to the pan and cook them in the sauce for a few more minutes.
4. Serve the Beef Steak Diane with a side of your choice.

BUTTER BEAN AND KALE STEW

Prep Time
10 mins

Cook Time
25 mins

Total Time
35 mins

Serving
4

Nutrition

Calories: 480 kcal, Protein: 22g,
Carbohydrate: 60g, Fat: 12g, Fiber: 16g

INGREDENTS

- 2 cans (15 oz each) of butter beans, drained and rinsed
- 4 cups chopped kale
- 2 cloves garlic, minced
- 1 onion, diced
- 4 cups vegetable broth
- Salt and pepper to taste

INSTRUCTIONS

1. In a large pot, sauté the onion and garlic until soft.
2. Add the kale and cook until wilted.
3. Add the butter beans, vegetable broth, salt, and pepper.
4. Simmer for 20 minutes.
5. Serve hot with a sprinkle of parmesan if desired.

BAKED TILAPIA WITH LEMON AND DILL

Prep Time
10 mins

Cook Time
20 mins

Total Time
30 mins

Serving
4

Nutrition

Calories: 480 kcal, Protein: 48g,
Carbohydrate: 2g, Fat: 30g, Fiber: 0g

INGREDENTS	INSTRUCTIONS
<ul><li>4 tilapia fillets (around 500g total)</li><li>2 tbsp olive oil</li><li>1 tbsp lemon juice</li><li>1 tbsp chopped fresh dill</li><li>Salt and pepper to taste</li></ul>	1. Turn your oven heat range to 375°F (190°C). 2. Rub the tilapia fillets with olive oil, lemon juice, dill, salt, and pepper. Place them in a baking dish. 3. Bake for 15-20 minutes until the tilapia is cooked and flakes easily with a fork. 4. Serve and enjoy.

LENTIL AND BARLEY SOUP

Prep Time
10 mins

Cook Time
40 mins

Total Time
50 mins

Serving
4

Nutrition

Calories: 440 kcal, Protein: 22g,
Carbohydrate: 78g, Fat: 2g, Fiber: 20g

INGREDENTS

- 1 cup lentils
- 1/2 cup barley
- 4 cups vegetable broth
- 2 carrots, diced
- 2 stalks of celery, diced
- 1 onion, diced
- 2 cloves garlic, minced
- Salt and pepper to taste

INSTRUCTIONS

1. In a large pot, sauté the onion, carrots, celery, and garlic until soft.
2. Add the lentils, barley, vegetable broth, salt, and pepper.
3. Simmer for 30-40 minutes or until lentils and barley are tender.
4. Serve hot.

BEEF AND MUSHROOM STROGANOFF

 Prep Time
20 mins

 Cook Time
30 mins

 Total Time
50 mins

 Serving
4

Nutrition

Calories: 480 kcal, Protein: 42g,
Carbohydrate: 8g, Fat: 30g, Fiber: 1g

INGREDENTS

- 500g lean beef strips
- 1 cup sliced mushrooms
- 1 cup sour cream
- Salt and pepper to taste

INSTRUCTIONS

1. Put the non-stick skillet over medium heat, cook the beef strips until browned. Remove from the skillet and set aside.
2. In the same skillet, sauté the mushrooms until softened.
3. Return the beef to the skillet and add the sour cream. Add, combine, and cook until heated thoroughly.
4. Season with salt and pepper to taste.
5. If desired, serve the Beef and Mushroom Stroganoff over whole-grain noodles or brown rice.

CHICKPEA AND QUINOA SALAD

 Prep Time
10 mins

 Cook Time
20 mins

 Total Time
30 mins

Serving
4

Nutrition

Calories: 420 kcal, Protein: 14g,
Carbohydrate: 56g, Fat: 14g, Fiber: 16g

INGREDENTS

- 2 cups cooked quinoa
- 2 cups cooked chickpeas
- 2 cups chopped cucumber
- 1 cup diced tomatoes
- 1/4 cup chopped fresh mint
- 1/4 cup chopped fresh parsley
- 3 tablespoons olive oil
- 2 tbsp lemon juice
- Salt and pepper to taste

INSTRUCTIONS

1. Combine the quinoa, chickpeas, cucumber, tomatoes, mint, and parsley in a large bowl.
2. Whisk the three tbsp olive oil with 2 tbsp lemon juice, salt, and crushed pepper in a small bowl.
3. Pour the lemon oil dressing over the salad and toss to combine.

BARBECUED SPICY CHICKEN WINGS

Prep Time
10 mins

Cook Time
30 mins

Total Time
40 mins

Serving
4

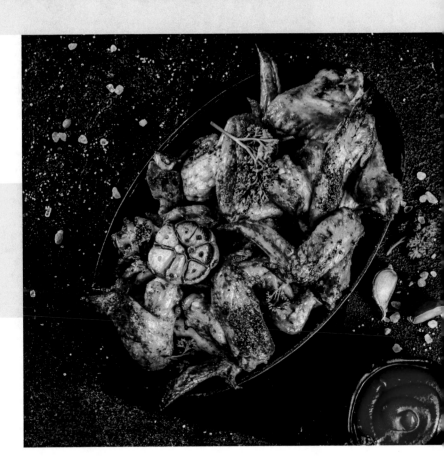

Nutrition

Calories: 410 kcal, Protein: 40g,
Carbohydrate: 20g, Fat: 18g, Fiber: 1g

INGREDENTS

- 500g chicken wings
- 1/2 cup barbecue sauce
- 1/2 tsp cayenne pepper
- Salt to taste

INSTRUCTIONS

1. Preheat your grill to medium heat.
2. Season the chicken wings with the cayenne pepper and salt.
3. Grill the wings for about 15 minutes per side or until cooked through.
4. Brush the wings with the barbecue sauce and grill for 5 minutes.
5. Serve the Barbecued Spicy Chicken Wings with a side of your choice.

ROASTED VEGETABLE AND FARRO SALAD

Prep Time
10 mins

Cook Time
25 mins

Total Time
35 mins

Serving
4

Nutrition

Calories: 430 kcal, Protein: 10g,
Carbohydrate: 62g, Fat: 16g, Fiber: 16g

INGREDENTS

- 2 cups cooked farro
- 2 bell peppers, diced
- 1 zucchini, diced
- 1 eggplant, diced
- 1/4 cup olive oil
- Salt and pepper to taste
- 1/4 cup balsamic vinegar
- 2 cups baby spinach

INSTRUCTIONS

1. Turn your oven heat range to 400°F (200°C).
2. Toss the bell peppers, zucchini, and eggplant with half of the olive oil, salt, and crushed pepper.
3. Spread on the oven sheet (in one layer) and roast for 23-25 minutes or until vegetables are tender.
4. Combine the cooked farro, roasted vegetables, and spinach in a large bowl.
5. Drizzle with the leftover olive oil and balsamic vinegar.
6. Toss to combine and serve.

ROAST BEEF WITH THYME AND ROSEMARY

Prep Time
10 mins

Cook Time
60 mins

Total Time
1 hrs 10 mins

Serving
4

Nutrition

Calories: 460 kcal, Protein: 50g,
Carbohydrate: 2g, Fat: 25g, Fiber: 1g

INGREDENTS

- 1 kg beef roast
- 2 tbsp olive oil
- 2 tbsp fresh thyme leaves
- 2 tbsp chopped fresh rosemary
- Salt and pepper to taste

INSTRUCTIONS

1. Turn your oven heat range to 375°F (190°C).
2. Rub the beef roast with olive oil, thyme, rosemary, salt, and crushed pepper.
3. Put the roast in a frypan and bake for 60 minutes until it reaches your desired level of doneness.
4. Rest the roasted be for 10 minutes before slicing and serving.

BROCCOLI, CHICKPEA, AND AVOCADO PITA SANDWICHES

Prep Time
10 mins

Cook Time
05 mins

Total Time
15 mins

Serving
4

Nutrition

Calories: 420 kcal, Protein: 17g,
Carbohydrate: 70g, Fat: 10g, Fiber: 16g

INGREDENTS

- 4 whole grain pita bread
- 2 cups cooked chickpeas
- 2 cups chopped broccoli
- 1 avocado, mashed
- 1/2 cup Greek yogurt
- Salt and pepper to taste

INSTRUCTIONS

1. Mix the mashed avocado, Greek yogurt, salt, and pepper in a bowl.
2. In another bowl, toss together the chickpeas and broccoli.
3. Cut a slit in each pita and spread the avocado mixture inside.
4. Fill with the chickpea and broccoli mixture.

CHICKEN PARMESAN

Prep Time
20 mins

Cook Time
30 mins

Total Time
50 mins

Serving
4

Nutrition

Calories: 410 kcal, Protein: 45g,
Carbohydrate: 10g, Fat: 20g, Fiber: 2g

INGREDENTS

- 4 chicken breasts (around 500g total)
- 1 cup marinara sauce
- 1/2 cup grated Parmesan cheese
- Salt and pepper to taste

INSTRUCTIONS

1. Turn your oven heat range to 375°F (190°C).
2. Put chicken breasts in the oven dish and season them with salt and pepper.
3. Spread the marinara sauce over the chicken, then sprinkle the Parmesan cheese.
4. Bake for 27-30 minutes until the chicken is done thoroughly, and the cheese melts completely and is golden.
5. Serve the Chicken Parmesan with a side of your choice.

PUMPKIN AND BEAN SOUP

Prep Time
10 mins

Cook Time
25 mins

Total Time
35 mins

Serving
4

Nutrition

Calories: 460 kcal, Protein: 17g,
Carbohydrate: 80g, Fat: 4g, Fiber: 21g

INGREDENTS

- 2 cans (15 oz weight) of white beans, drained and rinsed
- 1 can (15 oz) pumpkin puree
- 1 onion, diced
- 2 cloves garlic, minced
- 4 cups vegetable broth
- 1 tablespoon chili powder
- Salt and pepper to taste

INSTRUCTIONS

1. In a large pot, sauté the onion and garlic until soft.
2. Add the beans, pumpkin puree, vegetable broth, chili powder, salt, and pepper.
3. Put the pot gently boil and cook for 17-20 minutes.
4. If desired, pure half the soup with an immersion blender for a creamier texture.
5. Serve hot.

HIGH
FIBER
★★★

SEAFOOD PAELLA

Prep Time
30 mins

Cook Time
40 mins

Total Time
1 hrs 10 mins

Serving
4

Nutrition

Calories: 480 kcal, Protein: 45g,
Carbohydrate: 60g, Fat: 10g, Fiber: 5g

INGREDENTS

- 200g short-grain brown rice
- 300g mixed seafood (like shrimp, mussels, and calamari)
- 1 cup vegetable broth
- Salt and pepper to taste

INSTRUCTIONS

1. Put the skillet over medium heat, cook the rice in the vegetable broth until it is tender and the broth is absorbed.
2. Add the mixed seafood to the skillet and cook until it is cooked through.
3. Season the paella with salt and pepper to taste.
4. Serve the Seafood Paella with a side of your choice.

LENTIL AND WHOLE WHEAT PASTA SALAD

Prep Time
10 mins

Cook Time
20 mins

Total Time
30 mins

Serving
4

Nutrition

Calories: 410 kcal, Protein: 17g,
Carbohydrate: 67g, Fat: 9g, Fiber: 16g

INGREDIENTS

- 2 cups cooked whole wheat pasta
- 2 cups cooked lentils
- 2 cups chopped cucumber
- 1 cup diced tomatoes
- 1/4 cup chopped fresh mint
- 1/4 cup chopped fresh parsley
- 3 tablespoons olive oil
- Juice of 1 lemon
- Salt and pepper to tastet

INSTRUCTIONS

1. Combine the whole wheat pasta, lentils, cucumber, tomatoes, mint, and parsley in a large bowl.
2. Whisk the three tbsp olive oil with 1 lemon juice, salt, and crushed pepper in a small bowl.
3. Pour the lemon oil dressing over the salad and toss to combine.

HIGH
FIBER
★★★

SMOKED TURKEY BREAST

Prep Time
10 mins

Cook Time
2 hours

Total Time
2 hrs 10 mins

Serving
4

Nutrition

Calories: 400 kcal, Protein: 50g,
Carbohydrate: 0g, Fat: 20g, Fiber: 0g

INGREDIENTS

- 1 kg turkey breast
- 2 tbsp olive oil
- Salt and pepper to taste

INSTRUCTIONS

1. Turn your smoker heat range to 225°F (107°C).
2. Rub the meat breast with olive oil, salt, and crushed pepper.
3. Smoke the turkey for two hours until it almost touches the internal temperature of 165°F (74°C).
4. Rest the meat breast for 10 minutes before slicing and serving.

PEARL BARLEY AND VEGETABLE STIR-FRY

Prep Time
10 mins

Cook Time
25 mins

Total Time
35 mins

Serving
4

Nutrition

Calories: 400 kcal, Protein: 9g,
Carbohydrate: 70g, Fat: 9g, Fiber: 16g

INGREDIENTS

- 2 cups cooked pearl barley
- 2 bell peppers, diced
- 1 zucchini, diced
- 1 eggplant, diced
- 2 tablespoons olive oil
- 2 tablespoons soy sauce
- 1 tablespoon sesame oil
- Salt and pepper to tastet

INSTRUCTIONS

1. Heat two tbsp olive oil in a non-stick pan or wok over medium heat.
2. Add bell peppers, zucchini, eggplant, and stir-fry until vegetables are tender.
3. Add the cooked pearl barley, soy sauce, sesame oil, salt, and pepper.
4. Stir to combine and cook for three minutes.

HIGH
FIBER
★★★

GRILLED BEEF SKEWERS

Prep Time
15 mins

Cook Time
15 mins

Total Time
30 mins

Serving
4

Nutrition

Calories: 460 kcal, Protein: 50g,
Carbohydrate: 0g, Fat: 28g, Fiber: 0g

INGREDENTS	INSTRUCTIONS
• 600g lean beef cubes • 2 tbsp olive oil • Salt and pepper to taste	1. Preheat your grill to medium heat. 2. Thread the beef cubes onto skewers. Drizzle them with two tbsp oil, and season with salt and crushed pepper. 3. Grill the skewers for 3-4 minutes for the side until the beef is cooked to your liking. 4. Serve the Grilled Beef Skewers with a side of your choice.

VEGETABLE AND QUINOA STUFFED ZUCCHINI BOATS

Prep Time
15 mins

Cook Time
30 mins

Total Time
45 mins

Serving
4

Nutrition

Calories: 420 kcal, Protein: 13g,
Carbohydrate: 72g, Fat: 9g, Fiber: 15g

INGREDIENTS

- 4 zucchinis, halved lengthwise
- 2 cups cooked quinoa
- 1 bell pepper, diced
- 1 tomato, diced
- 1 onion, diced
- 1 clove garlic, minced
- 1 tablespoon olive oil
- Salt and pepper to taste

INSTRUCTIONS

1. Turn your oven heat range to 375°F (190°C).
2. Scoop out the inside of the zucchini halves to create a "boat."
3. Heat one tbsp olive oil in a non-stick pan and sauté the bell pepper, tomato, onion, and garlic until tender.
4. Add prepared quinoa and season with salt and crushed pepper.
5. Spoon the mixture into the zucchini boats.
6. Bake for 27-30 minutes until the zucchini is tender.

CHICKEN TERIYAKI

Prep Time
10 mins

Cook Time
20 mins

Total Time
30 mins

Serving
4

Nutrition

Calories: 420 kcal, Protein: 45g,
Carbohydrate: 15g Fat: 18g, Fiber: 0g

INGREDENTS

- 600g chicken breast
- 1/2 cup teriyaki sauce
- 1 tbsp olive oil
- Salt to taste

INSTRUCTIONS

1. Heat one tbsp oil in a non-stick skillet over medium heat.
2. Add chicken and cook until it the meat is done thoroughly.
3. Add teriyaki sauce over the chicken and stir to coat.
4. Simmer for a few minutes until the sauce has thickened slightly.
5. Serve the Chicken Teriyaki with a side of your choice.

CAULIFLOWER AND CHICKPEA CURRY

Prep Time
15 mins

Cook Time
30 mins

Total Time
45 mins

Serving
4

Nutrition

Calories: 470 kcal, Protein: 13g,
Carbohydrate: 60g, Fat: 23g, Fiber: 15g

INGREDIENTS

- 2 cups chopped cauliflower
- 2 cups cooked chickpeas
- 1 onion, diced
- 2 cloves garlic, minced
- 2 tablespoons curry powder
- 1 can (15 oz) diced tomatoes
- 1 can (13.5 oz) coconut milk
- 2 tablespoons olive oil
- Salt and pepper to taste

INSTRUCTIONS

1. Begin by warming olive oil in a sizable pan set at medium heat.
2. Once heated, introduce onion and garlic, sautéing them until they achieve a tender texture.
3. Follow this by incorporating curry powder into the pan and stirring until its aroma is released.
4. Next, mix cauliflower, chickpeas, diced tomatoes, coconut milk, salt, and pepper into the pan.
5. Transform the heat to a simmer, allowing the mixture to cook for about 20 to 30 minutes until the cauliflower softens.

BAKED LAMB SHANKS

Prep Time
10 mins

Cook Time
2 hours

Total Time
2 hrs 10 mins

Serving
4

Nutrition

Calories: 500 kcal, Protein: 50g,
Carbohydrate: 0g, Fat: 34g, Fiber: 0g

INGREDENTS	INSTRUCTIONS
• 4 lamb shanks • 2 tbsp olive oil • Salt and pepper to taste	1. Turn your oven heat range to 325°F (163°C). 2. Rub the lamb shanks with the olive oil, salt, and pepper. Place them in a roasting pan. 3. Bake the lamb shanks for about 2 hours. 4. Serve the Baked Lamb Shanks with a side of your choice.

CABBAGE AND WHITE BEAN STEW

Prep Time
10 mins

Cook Time
30 mins

Total Time
40 mins

Serving
4

Nutrition

Calories: 410 kcal, Protein: 18g,
Carbohydrate: 70g, Fat: 5g, Fiber: 17g

INGREDENTS	INSTRUCTIONS
• 4 cups chopped cabbage • 2 cans (15 oz weight) of white beans, drained and rinsed • 1 onion, diced • 2 cloves garlic, minced • 4 cups vegetable broth • 1 tablespoon olive oil • Salt and pepper to taste	1. Warm olive oil in a big pot on medium heat. 2. Toss in onion and garlic, and sauté till they soften. Add cabbage, white beans, vegetable broth, salt, and pepper. 3. Allow it to simmer, cooking for 20-30 minutes until the cabbage becomes tender.

HIGH
FIBER

BAKED HALIBUT WITH LEMON CAPER SAUCE

 Prep Time
10 mins

 Cook Time
20 mins

 Total Time
30 mins

 Serving
4

Nutrition

Calories: 430 kcal, Protein: 50g,
Carbohydrate: 4g, Fat: 22g, Fiber: 1g

INGREDENTS

- 800g halibut fillets
- 1 lemon, juiced
- 2 tbsp capers
- 2 tbsp olive oil
- Salt and pepper to taste

INSTRUCTIONS

1. Turn your oven heat range to 400°F (204°C).
2. Place the halibut fillets in a baking dish. Drizzle the halibut with the olive oil, and season with salt and pepper.
3. Bake the halibut for about 20 minutes or until it is flaky and cooked.
4. In a bowl, pulse the lemon juice with capers. Drizzle this sauce over the baked halibut.
5. Serve the Baked Halibut with Lemon Caper Sauce with a side of your choice.

BLACK BEAN AND SWEET POTATO ENCHILADAS

Prep Time
15 mins

Cook Time
25 mins

Total Time
40 mins

Serving
4

Nutrition

Calories: 500 kcal, Protein: 21g,
Carbohydrate: 80g, Fat: 12g, Fiber: 19g

INGREDENTS

- 8 whole grain tortillas
- 2 cups cooked and mashed sweet potato
- 2 cans (15 oz weight) of black beans, drained and rinsed
- 1 cup shredded cheese
- 1 jar (16 oz) enchilada sauce
- 1/2 cup chopped fresh cilantro

INSTRUCTIONS

1. Turn your oven heat range to 375°F (190°C).
2. In a bowl, mix the sweet potato and black beans.
3. Spread a layer (a thin) of enchilada sauce on the base of a baking dish.
4. Stuff each tortilla with the sweet potato, and black bean mixture, then roll it up and place seam-side down in the baking dish.
5. Top with the leftover enchilada sauce and sprinkle with cheese.
6. Bake for 23-25 minutes until the cheese melts completely.
7. Garnish with fresh cilantro before serving.

High Protein High Fiber Drinks

BERRY PROTEIN SMOOTHIE

Prep Time
05 mins

Cook Time
00 mins

Total Time
05 mins

Serving
1

Nutrition

Calories: 280 kcal, Protein: 23g,
Carbohydrate: 30g, Fat: 8g, Fiber: 12g

INGREDENTS

- 1 cup mixed berries
  (blueberries, strawberries,
  raspberries)
- 1 cup almond milk
- 1 scoop vanilla protein
  powder
- 1 tablespoon chia seeds

INSTRUCTIONS

1. Rinse your berries under cold water and pat dry. If using
   strawberries, remove the stems.
2. Add the berries to your blender, followed by the almond
   milk, protein powder, and chia seeds.
3. Blend on high power until you reach a smooth and creamy
   texture.
4. Pour into the serving glass and enjoy immediately for the
   best taste and texture.

MANGO LASSI WITH GREEK YOGURT

 Prep Time
05 mins

 Cook Time
00 mins

 Total Time
05 mins

 Serving
1

Nutrition

Calories: 290 kcal, Protein: 26g,
Carbohydrate: 45g, Fat: 3g, Fiber: 6g

INGREDENTS	INSTRUCTIONS
• 1 ripe mango, peeled and cubed • 1 cup Greek yogurt • 1 scoop vanilla protein powder • 1 tablespoon flax seeds	1. Begin by peeling your mango. Slice the flesh of the pit and chop it into cubes. 2. Add the mango cubes to your blender, followed by Greek yogurt, protein powder, and flax seeds. 3. Blend the ingredients on high until the mixture becomes completely smooth and creamy. 4. Pour the lassi into a glass, chill if desired, and enjoy.

GREEN POWER SMOOTHIE

Prep Time
05 mins

Cook Time
00 mins

Total Time
05 mins

Serving
1

Nutrition

Calories: 300 kcal, Protein: 23g,
Carbohydrate: 40g, Fat: 7g, Fiber: 10g

INGREDIENTS

- 1 cup spinach or kale
- 1 banana
- 1 cup almond milk
- 1 scoop vanilla protein powder
- 1 tablespoon chia seeds

INSTRUCTIONS

1. Place the spinach or kale into your blender.
2. Add the banana, almond milk, protein powder, and chia seeds.
3. Blend on high power until you reach a smooth and creamy texture.
4. Pour into a glass and serve immediately.

AVOCADO BERRY SMOOTHIE

Prep Time
05 mins

Cook Time
00 mins

Total Time
05 mins

Serving
1

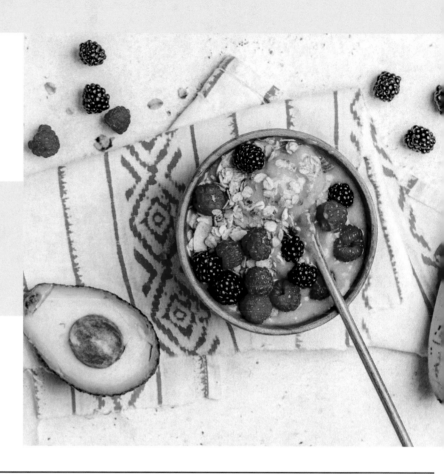

Nutrition

Calories: 320 kcal, Protein: 24g,
Carbohydrate: 30g, Fat: 15g, Fiber: 15g

INGREDENTS

- 1/2 avocado
- 1 cup mixed berries
- 1 cup almond milk
- 1 scoop vanilla protein powder
- 1 tablespoon flax seeds

INSTRUCTIONS

1. Slice the avocado to remove the pit and scoop out the flesh.
2. Add the avocado, mixed berries, almond milk, protein powder, and flax seeds to your blender.
3. Blend on a high-power setting until the mixture is completely smooth.
4. Pour into a glass and serve immediately.

PUMPKIN SPICE SMOOTHIE

Prep Time
05 mins

Cook Time
00 mins

Total Time
05 mins

Serving
1

Nutrition

Calories: 310 kcal, Protein: 24g,
Carbohydrate: 40g, Fat: 7g, Fiber: 11g

INGREDIENTS

- 1/2 cup pumpkin puree
- 1 banana
- 1 cup almond milk
- 1 scoop vanilla protein powder
- 1 tablespoon chia seeds
- 1/2 teaspoon pumpkin pie spice

INSTRUCTIONS

1. Add the pumpkin puree, banana, almond milk, protein powder, chia seeds, and pumpkin pie spice to your blender.
2. Blend on a high-power setting until the mixture is completely smooth.
3. Pour into a glass and serve immediately.

PROTEIN ICED COFFEE

Prep Time
05 mins

Cook Time
00 mins

Total Time
05 mins

Serving
1

Nutrition

Calories: 200 kcal, Protein: 25g,
Carbohydrate: 15g, Fat: 5g, Fiber: 10g

INGREDENTS	INSTRUCTIONS
<ul><li>1 cup brewed coffee, cooled</li><li>1 scoop of chocolate protein powder</li><li>1 cup unsweetened almond milk</li><li>1 tablespoon chia seeds</li></ul>	1. Combine coffee, protein powder, almond milk, and chia seeds in a blender. 2. Blend until smooth and frothy. 3. Pour over ice and serve.

VANILLA ALMOND SHAKE

Prep Time
05 mins

Cook Time
00 mins

Total Time
05 mins

Serving
1

Nutrition

Calories: 350 kcal, Protein: 30g,
Carbohydrate: 15g, Fat: 20g, Fiber: 10g

INGREDENTS	INSTRUCTIONS
• 1 scoop vanilla protein powder • 1 cup unsweetened almond milk • 1 tablespoon almond butter • 1 tablespoon chia seeds	1. In a blender, combine protein powder, almond milk, almond butter, and chia seeds. 2. Blend until smooth and creamy. 3. Pour into a glass and serve.

TURMERIC LATTE

Prep Time
05 mins

Cook Time
00 mins

Total Time
05 mins

Serving
1

Nutrition

Calories: 250 kcal, Protein: 30g,
Carbohydrate: 10g, Fat: 10g, Fiber: 5g

INGREDENTS	INSTRUCTIONS
• 1 cup unsweetened almond milk • 1 scoop vanilla protein powder • 1 teaspoon turmeric powder • 1 tablespoon flaxseeds	1. Heat the non-dairy milk almond milk in a saucepan until hot. 2. Pour into a blender with the protein powder, turmeric, and flaxseeds. 3. Blend until smooth and frothy. 4. Pour into a glass and serve warm.

HIGH PROTEIN HOT CHOCOLATE

Prep Time
05 mins

Cook Time
00 mins

Total Time
05 mins

Serving
1

Nutrition

Calories: 200 kcal, Protein: 25g,
Carbohydrate: 15g, Fat: 7g, Fiber: 10g

INGREDIENTS

- 1 cup unsweetened almond milk
- 1 scoop of chocolate protein powder
- 1 tablespoon unsweetened cocoa powder
- 1 tablespoon chia seeds

INSTRUCTIONS

1. Heat the non-dairy milk almond milk in a saucepan until hot.
2. Pour the protein powder, cocoa powder, and chia seeds into a blender.
3. Blend until smooth and frothy.
4. Pour into a glass and serve warm.

PROTEIN MOCHA

Prep Time
05 mins

Cook Time
00 mins

Total Time
05 mins

Serving
1

Nutrition

Calories: 250 kcal, Protein: 25g,
Carbohydrate: 20g, Fat: 7g, Fiber: 10g

INGREDENTS	INSTRUCTIONS
• 1 cup brewed coffee, cooled • 1 scoop of chocolate protein powder • 1 cup unsweetened almond milk • 1 tablespoon cocoa powder • 1 tablespoon chia seeds	1. Combine coffee, protein powder, almond milk, cocoa powder, and chia seeds in a blender. 2. Blend until smooth and frothy. 3. Pour into a glass and serve.

Dips, Hummus, And Suace Recipes

GREEK YOGURT AND DILL DIP

Prep Time
05 mins

Cook Time
00 mins

Total Time
05 mins

Serving
4

Nutrition

Calories: 70 kcal, Protein: 6g,
Carbohydrate: 4g, Fat: 3g, Fiber: 0g

INGREDIENTS

- 1 cup Greek yogurt
- 2 tablespoons chopped fresh dill
- 1 clove garlic, minced
- Salt and pepper to taste

INSTRUCTIONS

1. Combine Greek yogurt, dill, and garlic in a bowl.
2. Season with salt and pepper.
3. Stir until well combined.
4. Serve chilled with your favorite vegetables or pita bread.

SPICY RED PEPPER HUMMUS

Prep Time
10 mins

Cook Time
00 mins

Total Time
10 mins

Serving
4

Nutrition

Calories: 150 kcal, Protein: 6g,
Carbohydrate: 25g, Fat: 3g, Fiber: 6g

INGREDIENTS

- 1 can (15 ounces) chickpeas, rinsed and drained
- 1 roasted red bell pepper, peeled and chopped
- 2 cloves garlic, minced
- 1 tablespoon tahini
- Juice of 1 lemon
- Salt and pepper to taste
- A pinch of cayenne pepper

INSTRUCTIONS

1. Combine chickpeas, bell pepper, garlic, tahini, and lemon juice in a food processor.
2. Season with salt, pepper, and cayenne.
3. Blend until smooth.
4. Pour into the serving bowl and serve with your favorite vegetables or pita bread.

MINT AND POMEGRANATE RAITA

Prep Time
10 mins

Cook Time
00 mins

Total Time
10 mins

Serving
4

Nutrition

Calories: 80 kcal, Protein: 6g,
Carbohydrate: 9g, Fat: 3g, Fiber: 1g

INGREDIENTS	INSTRUCTIONS
• 1 cup Greek yogurt • 1/2 cup pomegranate seeds • 2 tablespoons chopped fresh mint • Salt and pepper to taste	1. Combine Greek yogurt, pomegranate seeds, and mint in a bowl. 2. Season with salt and pepper. 3. Stir until well combined. 4. Serve chilled with your favorite Indian dishes.

ROASTED GARLIC TZATZIKI

Prep Time
10 mins

Cook Time
00 mins

Total Time
10 mins

Serving
4

Nutrition

Calories: 60 kcal, Protein: 5g,
Carbohydrate: 5g, Fat: 2g, Fiber: 0g

INGREDENTS

- 1 cup Greek yogurt
- 1 cucumber, seeded and finely chopped
- 2 cloves roasted garlic, minced
- 1 tablespoon chopped fresh dill
- Salt and pepper to taste

INSTRUCTIONS

1. Combine Greek yogurt, cucumber, garlic, and dill in a bowl.
2. Season with salt and pepper.
3. Stir until well combined.
4. Serve chilled with your favorite Greek dishes.

AVOCADO AND CORN SALSA

Prep Time
10 mins

Cook Time
00 mins

Total Time
10 mins

Serving
4

Nutrition

Calories: 150 kcal, Protein: 3g,
Carbohydrate: 18g, Fat: 8g, Fiber: 6g

INGREDENTS

- 1 avocado, diced
- 1 cup corn kernels, fresh
- 1/2 cup diced red onion
- 1 jalapeño, seeded and finely chopped
- Juice of 1 lime
- Salt and pepper to taste

INSTRUCTIONS

1. Combine a bowl of avocado, corn, red onion, jalapeño, and lime juice.
2. Season with salt and pepper.
3. Stir until well combined.
4. Serve with tortilla chips with tacos or burritos.

GUACAMOLE WITH ROASTED GARLIC

Prep Time
10 mins

Cook Time
00 mins

Total Time
10 mins

Serving
4

Nutrition

Calories: 160 kcal, Protein: 2g,
Carbohydrate: 9g, Fat: 14g, Fiber: 7g

INGREDENTS

- 2 ripe avocados
- 2 cloves roasted garlic, minced
- 1 small onion, finely chopped
- Juice of 1 lime
- Salt and pepper to taste

INSTRUCTIONS

1. Mash the avocados in a bowl.
2. Add the roasted garlic, chopped onion, and lime juice.
3. Season with salt and pepper.
4. Stir until well combined.
5. Serve with tortilla chips with tacos or burritos.

BABA GANOUSH

Prep Time
10 mins

Cook Time
30 mins

Total Time
40 mins

Serving
4

Nutrition

Calories: 110 kcal, Protein: 3g,
Carbohydrate: 11g, Fat: 7g, Fiber: 5g

INGREDENTS

- 2 medium eggplants
- 2 cloves garlic, minced
- 2 tablespoons tahini
- Juice of 1 lemon
- Salt and pepper to taste

INSTRUCTIONS

1. Turn the oven heat range to 400°F (200°C) and arrange the baking sheet with foil.
2. Prick eggplants with a fork and place on the baking sheet.
3. Roast in the oven for thirty minutes or until soft.
4. Let cool, then scoop out the insides and place in a food processor.
5. Add the garlic, tahini, and lemon juice.
6. Season with salt and pepper.
7. Blend until smooth.
8. Serve with pita bread or vegetables.

MINT AND CORIANDER CHUTNEY

Prep Time
10 mins

Cook Time
00 mins

Total Time
10 mins

Serving
4

Nutrition

Calories: 10 kcal, Protein: 1g,
Carbohydrate: 2g, Fat: 0g, Fiber: 1g

INGREDENTS	INSTRUCTIONS
• 1 cup fresh mint leaves • 1 cup fresh coriander leaves • 1 green chili, chopped • Juice of 1 lemon • Salt to taste	1. Combine mint leaves, coriander leaves, chili, and lemon juice in a food processor. 2. Season with salt. 3. Blend until smooth. 4. Serve with Indian dishes or as a spread for sandwiches.

ROASTED RED PEPPER AND WALNUT DIP

Prep Time
10 mins

Cook Time
30 mins

Total Time
40 mins

Serving
4

Nutrition

Calories: 210 kcal, Protein: 5g,
Carbohydrate: 8g, Fat: 19g, Fiber: 3g

INGREDENTS

- 1 jar (12 ounces) of roasted red peppers, drained
- 1 cup walnuts
- 2 cloves garlic, minced
- Juice of 1 lemon
- Salt and pepper to taste

INSTRUCTIONS

1. Combine roasted red peppers, walnuts, garlic, and lemon juice in a food processor.
2. Season with salt and pepper.
3. Blend until smooth.
4. Serve with pita bread or vegetables.

SPINACH AND ARTICHOKE DIP

Prep Time
10 mins

Cook Time
20 mins

Total Time
30 mins

Serving
4

Nutrition

Calories: 210 kcal, Protein: 16g,
Carbohydrate: 10g, Fat: 12g, Fiber: 4g

INGREDENTS

- 1 can (14 oz weight) of artichoke hearts, drained and chopped
- 1 package (10 oz weight) of frozen spinach, thawed and drained
- 1 cup Greek yogurt
- 1 cup grated Parmesan cheese
- 1 clove garlic, minced
- Salt and pepper to taste

INSTRUCTIONS

1. Preheat oven to 350°F (175°C).
2. Combine the artichoke hearts, spinach, Greek yogurt, Parmesan cheese, and garlic in a bowl.
3. Season with salt and pepper.
4. Transfer the mixture to a baking dish.
5. Bake in the oven for about 20 minutes or until bubbly and golden.
6. Serve warm with pita bread or vegetables.

50+ MEAL
COMBO OPTIONS

Grilled Chicken Breast

EAT WITH

 → Black Bean and Vegetable Chili

 → Chickpea and Tomato Salad with Lemon Dressing

 → Vegetable and Quinoa Stuffed Zucchini Boats

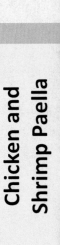 Greek Yogurt and Dill Dip

Beef Stir Fry with Rice

EAT WITH

 → Lentil and Vegetable Curry

 → Roasted Brussels Sprouts and Chickpea Salad

 → Chickpea and Quinoa Salad

Mint and Pomegranate Raita

Chicken and Shrimp Paella

EAT WITH

 → Avocado and Edamame Salad

 → Cauliflower and Chickpea Curry

 → Lentil and Whole Wheat Pasta Salad

 Baba Ganoush

Baked Lemon and Herb Salmon

 Beet and Lentil Salad

 Cauliflower Rice and Black Bean Burrito Bowl

 Pumpkin and Black Bean Soup

 Guacamole with Roasted Garlic

Lamb Meatballs Curry

 Three Bean Salad

 Mushroom and Brown Rice Risotto

 Roasted Sweet Potato and Quinoa Salad

 Roasted Garlic Tzatziki

Smoked Sea Bass with Herbs

 Brown Rice and Vegetable Stir-Fry

 Butternut Squash and Black Bean Stew

 Cabbage and White Bean Stew

 Roasted Red Pepper and Walnut Dip

Garlic Butter Baked Salmon

EAT WITH

Black Bean and Corn Salad

Chickpea and Broccoli Stir-fry

Broccoli and Brussels Sprouts Slaw

Avocado and Corn Salsa

Smoky BBQ Beef Brisket

EAT WITH

Apple, Walnut, and Mixed Greens Salad

Roasted Vegetable and Farro Salad

Cauliflower Fried Rice

Mint and Coriander Chutney

Soul Food Jerk Chicken

EAT WITH

Kidney Bean and Cabbage Slaw

Lentil and Whole Wheat Pasta Salad

Pearl Barley and Vegetable Stir-fry

Spicy Red Pepper Hummus

Baked Cod with Olive Tapenade

EAT WITH

 Lentil and Barley Soup

 Black Bean and Sweet Potato Enchiladas

 Vegetable and Quinoa Stuffed Zucchini Boats

 Spinach and Artichoke Dip

Chicken Souvlaki with Tzatziki Sauce

EAT WITH

 Black Bean and Vegetable Chili

 Vegetable and Black Bean Enchiladas

 Chickpea and Tomato Salad with Lemon Dressing

 Greek Yogurt and Dill Dip

Baked Chicken with Sun-Dried Tomato Cream Sauce

EAT WITH

 Lentil and Vegetable Curry

 Chickpea and Broccoli Stir-fry

 Roasted Brussels Sprouts and Chickpea Salad

 Mint and Pomegranate Raita

Baked Tilapia with Lemon and Dill

EAT WITH

 → Chickpea and Quinoa Salad

 → Cauliflower and Chickpea Curry

 → Avocado and Edamame Salad

Baba Ganoush

Beef and Mushroom Stroganoff

EAT WITH

 → Beet and Lentil Salad

→ Chickpea and Broccoli Stir-fry

 → Cauliflower Rice and Black Bean Burrito Bowl

Avocado and Corn Salsa

Chicken Parmesan

EAT WITH

 → Three Bean Salad

 → Baked Sweet Potato and Lentil Patties

→ Mushroom and Brown Rice Risotto

Guacamole with Roasted Garlic

Seafood Paella

Brown Rice and Vegetable Stir-Fry

Konjac Rice with Lentils and Vegetables

Butternut Squash and Black Bean Stew

Roasted Garlic Tzatziki

Chicken Teriyaki

EAT WITH

Mushroom and Spinach Cauliflower Risotto

Broccoli, Chickpea, and Avocado Pita Sandwiches

Black Bean and Corn Salad

Avocado and Corn Salsa

Barbecued Spicy Chicken Wings

EAT WITH

Lentil and Whole Wheat Pasta Salad

Pumpkin and Black Bean Soup

Apple, Walnut, and Mixed Greens Salad

Spicy Red Pepper Hummus

Baked Halibut with Lemon Caper Sauce

EAT WITH

Roasted Sweet Potato and Quinoa Salad

Cabbage and White Bean Stew

Kidney Bean and Cabbage Slaw

Spinach and Artichoke Dip

Roast Beef with Thyme and Rosemary

EAT WITH

Broccoli and Brussels Sprouts Slaw

Cauliflower Fried Rice

Pearl Barley and Vegetable Stir-fry

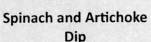

Roasted Red Pepper and Walnut Dip

CONCLUSION

Congratulations! You've reached the end of the High Protein-High Fiber Meal Prep Guide, and we hope this book has been a valuable resource in your journey towards a healthier and more fiber-rich diet. By incorporating the principles and recipes shared in this guide, you've taken a significant step towards improving your overall well-being.

Throughout this book, we've explored the importance of fiber in our diet and how it plays a crucial role in supporting digestion, promoting satiety, and maintaining a healthy weight. We've provided you with 100 delicious and nutritious recipes that are packed with fiber, ensuring that you never have to compromise on taste while prioritizing your health.

Meal prepping has been emphasized as a key strategy in this guide, and for a good reason. By dedicating a little time and effort upfront to plan and prepare your meals, you'll save time and stress during the week. Our Meal Prep Combos, featuring high-protein recipes paired with three high-fiber recipes, have been carefully curated to help you achieve a balanced and satisfying meal plan.

Remember, the journey to a healthier lifestyle is not about perfection but progress. Each small step you take towards incorporating more fiber-rich foods into your meals counts. Whether you choose to meal prep for the entire week or start with a few days, the important thing is that you're making conscious choices to prioritize your health.

As you continue your high-fiber meal prep journey, don't forget to listen to your body's needs and adjust the recipes to suit your taste preferences and dietary requirements. Feel free to experiment, add your favorite herbs and spices, and make these recipes your own.

We encourage you to make this book a handy reference guide, coming back to it whenever you need inspiration, new ideas, or a reminder of the benefits of a high-fiber diet. Share these recipes with your friends and loved ones, and together, create a community that prioritizes wellness and supports each other on the path to a healthier lifestyle.

We want to express our gratitude for joining us on this journey. Your commitment to improving your health through nutrition is commendable, and we hope this book has served as a valuable tool in your quest for a fiber-rich diet.

Remember, it's the small, consistent steps that lead to lasting change. Embrace the power of fiber, savor the delicious flavors, and nourish your body with every bite. Here's to a vibrant, energetic, and fiber-filled life!

Wishing you health and happiness,

Made in United States
North Haven, CT
19 June 2024

53807788R00069